# CONTENT

<u>Chapter</u>　　　　<u>Lesson Name</u>　　　　<u>Page No.</u>

# HISTORY OF NEURO PLASTICITY (NP)

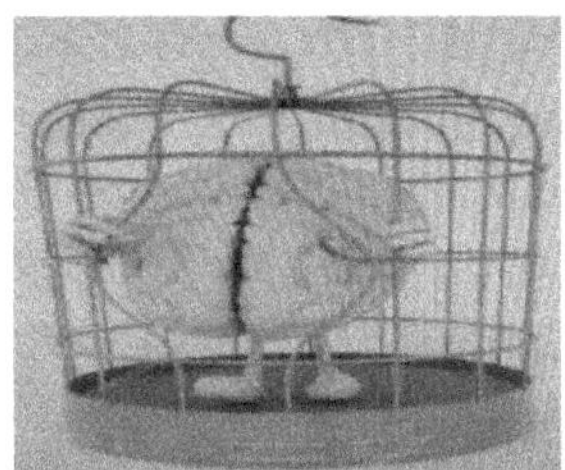 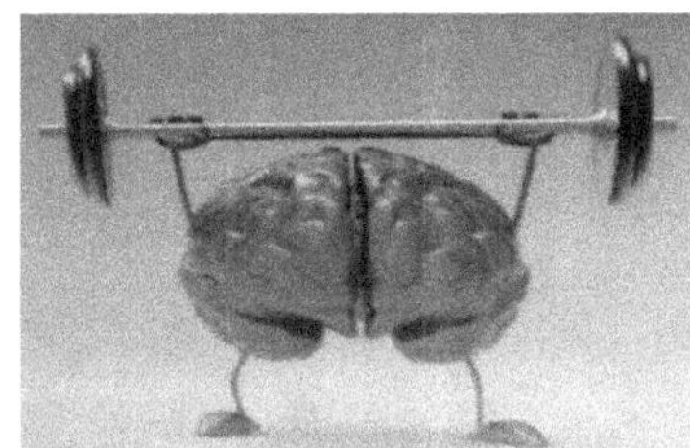

Neuro Plasticity was first coined by Polish scientist Jerzy Konorski in his book 'Integrative Activity of the Brain', published on 03.05.167. Demarin, Morovic and Bone In 2014 registered as father of Neuro Science. Dr. Richard Blender discovered about three Layers of human brain, he proved that human brain consist of three layers. The 1st layer is called Conscious, the 2nd layer is called as sub-conscious, and the 3rd layer is known as unconscious mind.

Conscious Mind: The human conscious mind consists of 15% Of total brain capacity. It belongs to right part of our brain. It just receipts the current happenings in our brain and within fraction of a second the message passes to our sub-conscious mind that place on the left side of our brain part. Hence, when we meet an old friend or a family member or a new member around us, we create a very fresh thought about the person.

Sub-conscious Mind: Our sub-conscious mind plays a vital role to influence our future as it consists of 65% our total brain power. When the message received from the conscious mind, the sub-conscious mind co-relate all past happenings with the person and create a new negative or positive thought about the said person or object, and direct our analytical conscious brain to analyze about the person and deal accordingly. Hence our conscious brain changes its mode of analyzing about the person. In one case, when I visited my family and friends in Odisha after 30 long years of my stay in Delhi, most of them were carrying my images of 30 years back, and most of them not recognized by my facial expression till I spoke few words to them. This is the classic example of how our conscious and sub-conscious brain functions. On the very next moment our subconsciousmind erases our past memory and record our present image for future references. This auto system of mind is called as Neuro Plasticity. Through these techniques the Neuro Plasticity experts can able to bring huge change inside human brain by which past memories of negativity, sufferings, pain and phobias those have been nested inside our brain since our childhood, that act as stumble block of our future prospect, stamping us as failure, useless, worthless, and  so many such negative titles conferred our parents, relatives, friends, and whole of the world around us, shall bring change completely.

Unconscious Mind: Our unconscious mind plays a vital role in changing records of our sub-conscious mind. This part of brain though consists of 20% of total brain memory, either it makes or breaks a person's life. This part of brain connects to our soul (the invincible GPS-like device) that has been installed inside our body alongside our heart. Our soul is the real rider of our chariot-like body, where as our limbs are the wheels, and our 5 sense organs are the five horses those drives the chariot that has been rein by our sub-conscious mind, but under direction of the rider(soul). But vary few people, with divine knowledge empowered (Siddha Himalayan Yogies) can know maneuvering of five sense elements by regular practicing of meditation that drive our life on right karmic path.

# WHAT IS NEURO PLATICITY (NP)?

**What is the meaning of Neuro Plasticity?**: Neuro - means nerve systems that comprise of one hundred billion neurons around our memory gland called amygdala placed on the back side of our brain that often directs 120 trillion of our blood cells, spread across our body, for action.

Plasticity - means the way we change our body or facial shape, in order to give our body the most attractive look (mostly celebrities do). Through intense practice, one can transform negative commands of our neurons connected to our sub-conscious brain and get positive outcome.

<u>Our mind receives instructions by five different senses</u> :

1. Visual, 2. Auditory, 3. Kinesthetic, 4. Smell and 5. Test.
1.  Visual: All visible matters by our eye comes under visual;
2.  All sound matters by our ears fall in auditory;
3.   Kinesthetic: All feelings maters by our skin around our body fall in kinesthetic;
4.  Smell: All smell using our nose like sweet flavor, odor, etc. fall in category of smell.
5.  Tests: Using our tongue like sweet, sour etc. are fall in category of taste;

Our brain mostly perceives and react through the above five senses. For example, if we visited to a party like wedding, birth day, marriage anniversary, etc. we mostly unknowingly come across use of all these five senses to perceive others good or bad reactions towards us. Like others mood of speaking perceived by our ear, viewing all actions by our eye, feeling ones way of touching, smelling the flavor of food, and testing the dishes by our mouth to consider about the quality of party and the friend recorded by our mind.

# Chapter-3

> <u>Internal Representational System :</u>
> ⬇
> <u>State of Mind  : Thoughts & Moods</u>
> ⬇
> <u>Resourceful / Positive  &   Un-resourceful / Negativities</u>

<u>Resourceful or Positive state of mind:</u>

Feel Confident, happy, flexible, etc.

<u>Un-resourceful / Negative state of mind:</u>

Feel Depression, anger, illness, frustration, Etc.

1. If we change our actions by programming our internal memory 

2. Our state of Mind changes to our behavior ⟹

3. Our behavior or attitude become our result ⟹

4. Finally our result becomes our destiny.


<u>How our brain receives data and converts into results?</u>


1. Thalamus: A part on our brain receives our information from our 5 sensory organs – eye, ear, nose, mouth and skin, and passes to sensory cortex.

2. Sensory cortex: interpret the received sensory data.

3. Hippocampus: Not only stores, but also quickly co-relates to similar past events to respond to stimuli.
4. Amygdala: Quickly interpret emotions and quickly advice for action.

5. Hippocampus: Releases adrenaline hormone to observe potential threat and decide either to fight or flight.

For example, when we see a tiger on the forest, our brain sense the mood of the tiger. And  sense whether it comes towards us to eat us up, then our brain direct us to flight from the scene and save ourselves. Or when our brain sense that the tiger is just pass by the side as it's stomachache is already full, our brain direct us not to worry, just stay safe.

# Chapter-4

# TEN MAJOR FOBIAS

We can overcome our 10 major phobias (% of affected persons globally) by using Nuro Plasticity Practice:

1.  Fear of death (20%) people are suffering: People fear to face death just because it is a natural phenomenon, the divine principles of God.

2.  Fear of loss of autonomy (5%): Most people feel unsecure of independentness.

3.  Fear of separation (4%): Most of us fear of separation from our dear ones during shifting to fare away places in case of marriage,  service, etc.

4.  Acrophobia (5%): Fear of falling from the height.

5.  Astraphobia (3%): Abnormal fear of thunder, cloud lightening, and adverse weather condition.

6.  Agoraphobia (9%): Between age group of 30s to adolescent fear stricken by crowded fights, terror attacks, warlike situations.

7.  Arachnophobia (3.5%): Unreasonable fear of spiders and other arachnids. Reasonable fear of spider, scorpion, and other arachnid.

8. Aerophobia (2.6%): Unusual fear of flying , airplane travel, parachuting, etc., even if there is no impending danger.

9. Cynophobia (9%): Fear of dogs. It can be disruptive or can continue to grow up to adulthood.

10. Mysophobia (2%): Fear of dirt. People from advanced countries maintain high level of hygiene mostly associated with such phobia. People habituated with high level of cleanliness often avoid places, areas, activities, that can cause contamination, especially during pandemics.

# Chapter-5

# TIMELINE OF LIFE - PRESENT, PAST AND FUTURE

Past good events recollection, exercise-1:

1. Recollect all happy, memorable and successful events happened in the past.
2. Fix them on the left hand tightly with nut and bolt. Look them daily after getting up from the bed and once more before going to bed.
2. Follow these happy moments and affirm to recreate the same enjoyable moments in near future.

Fist punch, exercise-2:

To overcome any phobia before going to exam hall, attending an interview, and so on, just stay astride, look to the blue sky for few second confidently, say you, "I am

(Your Name...), and I am confident of doing excellent on the (name of the job you going to perform...). Utter this seven times. Then create your right fist firm and punch on the left palm and hold tightly by your left palm for few seconds. This will build enormous inner confident within you.

# HOW DO OUR MEMORY FUNCTIONS?

On the back of our brain a tiny Memory Gland placed, called Amygdala: This small part store and dispense of our memory bank coiled by one hundred billion neurons. Each neuron has the capacity of 8 GB of memory storage. Total brain data storage on three layers- 1$^{st}$ is layer is called analytical brain. This data bank stores data for temporary period and having capacity of 15% of total data capacity of our brain. The 2$^{nd}$ layer of data stored in sub-conscious brain. When we repeatedly memorize or put stress on a particular subject our conscious brain send that data to sub-conscious layer of our brain for future reference. This layer contains around 65% of our total memory capacity of our brain. Our 3$^{rd}$ layer of data stored on unconscious brain. This layer stores around 20% of our total brain memory. This layer contains even oldest data that has not been used by our sub-conscious brain since a long time. Like the events of childhood or sometimes even previous life  memory comes with our Deoxyribonucleic Acid (DNA), which is completely connected to our karmic actions taken in previous life.

Hence, though we born from same parents get the same nourishment but, our way of lifestyle differ from other family members. This layer of memory remains unreadable and concealed like the divine principles of the creator. For example, why some people chooses life of a terrorist or criminal act? This is because, when we, selfish human being, for self comfort, ransacked nature's ethereal, areal and aquatic treasure, and extinguish all creature of forest, water and air, for expansion of human base. Hence, all the souls of wild creatures are entered into human bodies, but due to DNA of the previous acts of blood thirsty nature, become engaged into terrorists and other criminal activities.

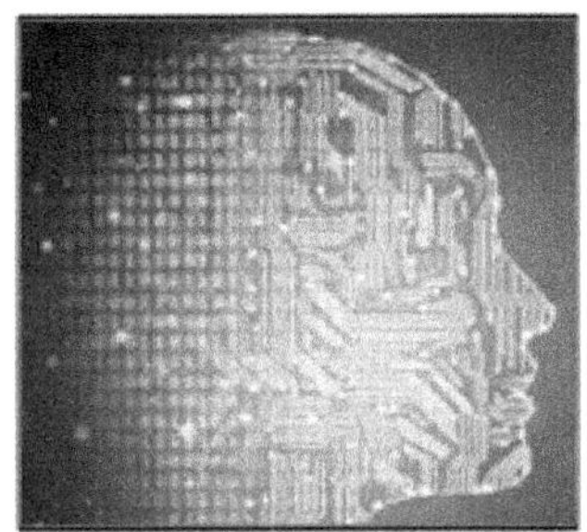

# Chapter-7

# PHYSICAL ASPECTS OF HUMAN BRAIN

Human brain is secured under scalp (a hard cover) on outer parts of our brain. Human brain weighs around 1.4 kg which is 2% of our total body weight. Our head functions like a divine computer- brain works like hardware and mind like software. In physical sense human brain can be divided into three parts- 1. Brain stem, 2. Cerebellum, and 3. Cerebrum.

Brain stem:  The Brain Stem seats atop of our spinal code. It has three nerve centers – the midbrain, pons and medulla oblongata. Midbrain helps control movements of the eye. The pons links the hemispheres of the cerebrum. The medulla regulates breathing, heartbeat and blood flow. In a nutshell, we can say that the stem takes care of the survival mechanism of our body.

Cerebellum: The cerebellum is located on the hind part of human brain and manages the movement of our body. Hence, it is called kinesthetic or muscle memory. Most athletics and sports persons are the master user of such memory.

<u>Cerebrum</u>: The cerebrum is the final and most important part of brain. It handles software functions of the brain. The cerebrum further divided into four lobes. A) The frontal lobe deals with problem solving. B) The parietal lobe helps process of information from the senses. C) The occipital lobe controls vision. D) The temporal lobe that controls memory, hearing and language. Apart from the above four types of functions, the cerebrum also handles two more important functions. The neocortex handles thought process and the limbic system handles the feeling process. The limbic system lets the mind meet the body, where the endocrine system interfaces with the brain. When the limbic system is well developed, intellectual and emotional aspect of life appears on our mind.

The Limbic again divided into five parts- Hippocampus, Amygdala, Hypothalamus, Thalamus, and Pituitary.

a. Hippocampus stores short term memories, and transfer all long term memories to the neocortex.

b. Amygdala stores all emotional memories, but when there is deep emotional impact, it shift to long term memories. Hence, emotion plays crucial role in long term memory. When strong emotions is involved, not forgotten for a long time.

c. Hypothalamus plays the role of a message centre between body and mind. Message sent through hormones. It controls body temperature, hunger and sexual functions. In the time of crisis it releases adrenaline hormones to decide either fight or flight from the event.

d. Thalamus deals with all incoming messages from our five sensory organs except test, and transmits them to the concerned processing centers in our brain. It works like a message transmitting centre in human brain.

e. Pituitary gland acts like an assistant to Hypothalamus in transmitting message and produce hormones in response to various situations. Hence it is also called as third eye or intuitive centre of human brain.

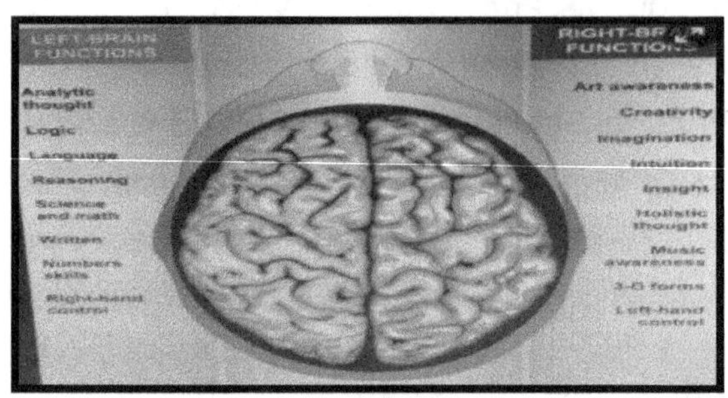


# Chapter-8

# FUNCTIONS OF LEFT AND RIGHT BRAIN

## Functions of Left Brain:

The thought process of left brain are: a) logical, b) linear, c) orderly, d) rational, e) sequential, f) organized, g) systematic H) reality based, i) dealing with abstract ideas, j) verbal expression, k) reading, l) writing, m) auditory, n) identifying facts and figures, o) phonetics and symbolism, and p) micro approach.

## Functions of Right Brain:

The thought process of right brain are a) creative, b) imaginative, c) random, d) intuitive, e) non-verbal ways of working, f) unorganized, g) spatial awareness, h) shape and pattern recognize, i) art, j) music, k) color sensitivity, l) feeling of presence of objects and people, m) visualization, and n) macro approach.

For extraction of optimum brain performance, both parts of brain given equal importance, and maintain perfect balance of both parts extract genius result in life.


<u>Ways to maintain balance in left and right brain:</u>
Earlier the believe was that the task on our hand dominance a particular side of our brain, but now it is clear that while in deep meditation or intense creativity, both hemispheres being produce the same type oOf brain waves in a single, coherent rhythm, operating in unison and produce the genius performance for us.


<u>Through external stimuli brain activities can be also altered and shaped:</u>
Recent search reveals that it is possible to create any kind of mental state like euphoria, recall past experiences, sexual excitement, deep concentration and heightened creativity by triggering specific sounds, lights, and electromagnetic fields.

Modern advanced scientific equipments can control our own thoughts, emotions, moods and mental state, at will. With help of such advanced equipments one can absorb, store, process, and recall vast amounts of information. Hence, now it is quite possible to intervene in the mind and memory on a physical level.

# Chapter-9

# How our Conscious and sub conscious mind functions (DDG)?

Suppose in our group tour, we visited Taj Mahal, one of the seven wonders of the universe, or Eiffel Tower in Paris. On return, if we asked to explain about the monument, I am sure, each one will give a different way of opinion. This is because our brain receives data in Delete, Distortion and Generalizing (DDG) format. Our brain records memory in Visual, Auditory and Kinesthetic (VAK) format. Our DNA develop our memory interest though either by seeing videos or pictures; by listening to sound; or by feeling by touching the object. Hence our brain quickly memories the single or multiple parts in which we Habituated to memorize. This is why, each of us express in a different perception about the same object. Many a time, we even distort the real importance to create extra importance about the object. Our brain record of the part of the event, we take interest in and delete the other points of the object. Many a time, when we meet a new friend, we keenly observe his or her actions and expressions. But, when we meet the same person again and again, we miss the same importance of observing actions and expressions, this is because we generalize our perception about his/her repeated behavior.

# Chapter-10

# How our believe system works?

We nurture numerous believes in our mind. Some of them are based on universal truth that believe by mass population of the globe, sometimes we develop some believes based on our own perception, are called as internal believe. Such believes changes in due course of time, but universal remains unchangeable for ever are called principles of divinity.

Our system of believes develop from the family, environment, education, an culture we live in. The thoughts we witness very often become saved in our sub-conscious mind, they gradually change into habits, then into our strong believe and open our way towards our destiny. This process takes long time and installed in our brain, remains for ever with us, until we take strong step to rectify it. This corrective process of our believe system is called Neuro Plasticity.

# Ways to treat a psych patient- Modality – [Event-1] & Sub-modality – [Event-2]

In NP find Modalities and sub-modalities of a person to Re-correct ones psychic problem. Modality means events or incidents in original state is called as **event-1**, and events in changed or distorted form saved on memory is called as sub-modality or **event-2**. To synchronize the state of mind of a psychic person to its original state is called as

Pre-supposition: All modalities and sub-modalities of a psychic person can be extracted by video, audio and kinesthetic (VAK) question format.

All answers of the question on event-1 (the original incident) to be matched with the event-2 ( the distorted responses) already nested on the mind of the psychic person, for which he/she has been suffering from such problem. Now we need to change the event -2 statements to equate the original statements of event-1 using many ways of treatment techniques like TV technique – Chapter-9, and Color cleansing technique-10, etc.

<u>Question format to examine a psychic patient,</u>
<u>Visual Questions</u>:
1. Is the event happened was in Movie or Still Picture Format?
2. Is it in Color or B&W?
3. Bright, dim or dark?
4. Right, Left or Centre?
5. Panoramic or framed view?
6. Up, down or Middle side?
7. Life Size, Normal or small in size?
8. 3D or2D view?
9. Close or Fare image?
10. Motion of image Fast, slow or medium?
11. Are you within the movie or watching from outside?
12. Any color impact you like the most?

<u>Auditory Questions</u>:
1. Is there any sound?
2. Are you saying something?

3. How Laud is the sound?
4. What is the part of in tour body sound is feeling it?
5. 5.   What is the frequency of sound – fast, medium or slow?
6. Where is the sound comes from – nearby or from fare away place?
7. Is the sound regular or irregular?
8. Is certain words in the sound emphasized,  certain importance of words?
9. How long the sound last – tome duration?
10. What's unique about this sound?
11. Anything create strong feeling or reaction on this sound?
12. Any special remark about this sound?

<u>Kinesthetic or Feeling questions</u>:

1. Breathing- high, low, or medium (normally 100 to 80 bits per minute, during run & exercise, or fear breathing even raise to 120 bits per minute)
2. Feeling located in the part of body?
3. Texture – rough or smooth?
4. Intensity- High or low?
5. Texture of breathing- Harsh or smooth?
6. Weight heavy or light?
7. Temperature of body – hot, cold or normal?
8. 8.Duration of feeling- long, short, or continua, discontinue?

9.  9.Movement direction- left, right, above or lower parts of body?

10. 1o.If movement – clockwise or anti-clockwise?

11. Any special effects that impact on mind?

12. Any other remarks?

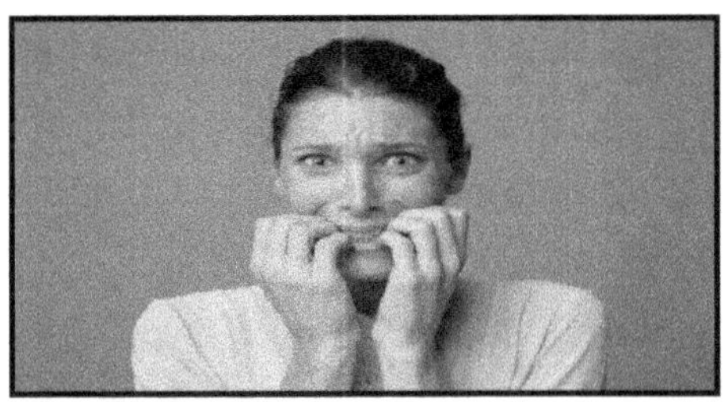

# Chapter-12

# TECHNIQUE OF REMOVING
# PAST BAD MEMORIES
# USING VAK QUESTIONS

Most of us suffered from past painful memories and phobias that nested inside our brain even unknown to us. But on experiencing similar situations in our life our sub -conscious brain, within no time, brings those incidents in into our mind, and recreates past events. The same painful memory, that creates stumble block in our future performance.

Following some NP techniques one can cleanse such fear or phobias from our brain those nested since time and events unknown to us.

TV Technique Exercise: (For example) - If some female have suffered from bitter misunderstanding with husband, due to some past family fight, and not able to reconcile with husband's past behavior, though husband repented for his guilty and assured not to repeat the same in future. In such case, the following TV Technique can help to wipe out the deep scare created inside the sub-conscious brain. Just imagine inside your brain that an obsolete old (b & w) TV is lying uselessly inside home. Any dirty table occupying your house uselessly. Just imagine, get the Dirty table and keep the (TV) set on the table. Open the set watch the old b & w  film song, turn the vision of the (TV) into black, slow down the volume of the (TV), now put some petrol took out from bike or car of your husband. Look the (TV) burnt on fire and turned into ashes. Look the ashes flew on tornado through the window of your drawing-room and oblivion into the cloud.

Now, replace your drawing room with a new designed table and brand new colorful TV set, a nice decorative flower pot alongside of the new TV set. Open the TV set and open your most favorite serial, Song or film. Watch the TV with happy and joy. Your husband enter with nice cuppa of tea or coffee to greet you. Sense the happiness returns back into your life. All the past fear dissolves into oblivion.

# Removing past anxiety
# Exercise using VAK Question

If you are suffered from deep anxiety due to your last failure in the class or competitive exam, and such fear of failure haunt you whenever you  try for the same competition in future. Just do the following exercise.

(For example) – $1^{st}$ of all using VAK question find the color of your fear of failure contains, the texture of the color contains- rough or smooth, etc. If the color of your fear had happened on a cloudy weather, you always feel cloudy color with the feelings of the similar incidents, and so on. Then imagine: You have gone to a picnic with your friends or family members to a natural water fall spot. You daubed your body with the same color, on your body that associated with the incident of failure. And set under the Water-fall. Imagine, the pressure flow of water washes away all the color from your body. Just imagine you are enjoying the water fountain and the color washing away from your body. As the complete color wash away, come out and dry your wet body and find no more color remain over any part of your body. This imagines represent wipe out of your past painful memories.

<u>Remove past sound anxiety Exercise</u>:

Many a time we feel some absurd type of sound in our throat, chest, stomach or any other parts of our body, that cause due to anxiety within our mind. If such sound feel on the throat or chest, ask the patient to move the opposite hand it appears and towards opposite direction. For example, ask the patient to use right hand if the sound feel left side of the body, and move gently towards the shoulder, move bellow if the sound feel upper side of the body and vice versa. So move from shoulder towards ankle of the hand, again move towards the thumb, talk to the sound with some funny language like with tone of funny actors like Rajpal Yadav, Jonny Liver, Jimmy Kerry, etc. Then ask the patient imagine asking a succession pump and putting the thumb on the succession nozzle to suck the sound and discard into oblivion.

Just after finishing this exercise, feel the level of relax from fear of anxiety.

# Switch Technique to Remove Uncomfortable Memories from Mind

Find the uncomfortable situations in life that creates stumble block in future growth using VAK question in event-1. Also find the favorable situation or image wish to change.

For Example: Follow these bellow mentioned steps.

1. If the psychiatric person wish to be a world class rich person like Bill Gets. Ask him/her questions using VAK format. Note down all the minus points inside himself.

2. Also ask the positive points of Bill Gets he knows for which become so wealthy.

3. Ask to frame a picture of both self and Bill Gets. Put the self made negative frame on the left palm, and the frame of Bill Gets on the right palm. Concentrate both the frame for few seconds, keeping both hands on left and right side, and

imagine how upset with self frame and how attractive the imaginary frame of Bill Gets is. Put the left palm with self frame in front of your eye and in few seconds slide counting 3210 slide the right palm over the left frame. And remove your left hand just after replacing right hand.

Repeat this exercise just before getting up from the bed once in the morning and just before going to the bed in the night. Repeat for 7 days with full faith saying that you are getting some changes inside your brain. Your brain is adopting Bill Gates's way of life function and some improvements happening inside you too.

# Chapter-15

# Exercise of Building inner Confident

Just list positive expects that cause lack of your inner confident, and be sure that after attaining those elements you will be unstoppable in achieving your goal of life. Now imagine you create babul balls as many as the list of your points of confidents those you lack within you. And be sure that once these confidents entered into your mind, you will win your dream goal. Now, put your points of confident in each babul ball and let them fly around your head within the semi-lighted room your enjoying alone. Observe those airy babul balls swirling around your head. Now count 321&0 and those babul balls burst after heating your head and the points of confident start entering inside your brain. Now look at the double quantity of babul balls appear automatically swaying around your head. Now again count 321&0 and look all the balls hit your head and burst. As soon as they get burst your confident level raise to double. Now, look 100s of such confident pill filled babul balls start swirling around your head. Start counting 321&0 and look they hit your head and burst. Now again look at them thousands in numbers of babul balls appear and hovering

around your head. Now count 321&0, they come and heat your head and the level of confident thousand times inside you. For last time look at these airy balls in millions of numbers. Now count 321&0 and feel the millions of confident balls hit your mind and, now become millions time confident to do your job perfectly.

# Chapter-16

# How to stay away from negative comments from environment?

Mostly we feel depressed, moral down on getting into our mind from family at home, friends, at work place, political parties, bureaucrats, etc. In such case, to keep such negative affects at bay, one needs to follow this technique. This is known as Air Balloon Technique.

For Example, before going to any meeting, or after getting exam result, many such negative and positive comments darted towards us from our family, friends, distant relatives, and so on. In such circumstances just imagine yourself placed inside an air balloon filled with cool oxygen, peace and most safety place, away from all negative environments. The skin of the air balloon is so thick that no word of negative comment reaching to your year. Only positive and cheering reactions of your known ones only could enter to you. Practicing this exercise you will succeed to overcome all negative and opposing attitude of your known crowd. Indian PM Mr. Narendra Damodar Midi, the master practioner of such exercise.

# Chapter-17

# How to change a negative person to a positive?

Changing a negative person into positivity is the function of God and Godly (incarnated) persons. For example, Lord Ram, Lord Krishna, Lord Jesus Christ, Prophet Muhammad, and so on, are not the real God. They just incarnated in human form just to teach the human being to become live a positive life leaving the path of negativity.

Even Mahtma Gandhi, Sorajini Naidu, Mother Teressa, Ravindra Nath Tagore, Dalai Lama and so on, are considered as incarnation of God. As Jesus Christ uttered, "Oh God! Forgive them, they don't know what they are doing", instead of protecting self, Christ tried to cleanse the sin the perpetrators were nailing Him, which made Christ as incarnation of God.

So, changing negativity in others is a divine task, and a very rare people can achieve such opportunity in life. This is why learning NP techniques with intention to sowing seed of positivity that bring change in some one is the real divine task. Just to earn money, distorting the facts playing the shortcut game is not beneficial for practicing this course. Because, this subject deal with 100% faith on divinity, own performance by practicing meditation for few minutes after awake from the bed and before going to the bed to stay mentally fit and fine, before advising else to change inside. (The details on this subject has been described in my e-book titled, "**Inner Voice**", available on Amazon Kindle Store at all sales centre across the globe.

# Chapter-18

# HOW TO GET RELIEF FROM OBSESSIVE COMPULSIVE DISORDER (OCD) ADDICTIVE?

Before providing treatment to any person suffering from OCD, just focus on following six points.

1. Challenge identity: How important is the person to the society?
2. Permission from sub-conscious mind: If the person mentally ready to get the treatment?
3. Try to find positive intention of the person suffering such disease / behavior.
4. Look at the person's creative mind and ask him following 4 questions:

a) How long the person suffering from this problem?

b) If he really wish to get rid of such problem?

c) Shall he/she wish to bring change in life by getting rid of from such addictive habits.

d) Is he/she ready to adopt a new habit in lieu of current suffering-ful habit?

5. Disease/behavioral acceptance from above 4 steps.

6. Life Balance: After verified by $5^{th}$ step, pass on to $6^{th}$ step for final certification by scrutinizing about perfection of the change to be made on patient's mind. If there is no side effect.

   For example, if the person wish to give-up chewing tobacco, or alcohol, but wish to take sugary foods like toffees, ice creams, etc. which may cause diabetes in long run. In such case again refer to 4 points on $4^{th}$ step to reconfirm, as long as a positive alternative is not come out for permanent eradication of such problem, do repeat the steps.

# REMOVE PROCESS OF DEPRESSION AND SUICIDAL TENDENCIES

Such deadly mental feelings comes to mind after long failure in our achievements in life. Our long depressive state of mind slowly and steadily feed to our brain neurons that no more success or positive result is available. Such chronic scar negatively insulates our neurons and presents a dark vision in front of our thoughts. Compel us to addict some way or other to get instant relief from such brain hammering negative thoughts. Though the addictive substances cut off our neurons' connectivity with our brain for some moments and send us to deep slumber, and we feel momentary relief, in long run, such substances act as poisonous for our body and mind. In spite of the past achievements, only cloudy negative images present to our brain. After long desperation force us to leave such painful life and find ways to escaping from life by way of suicide.

Mostly the reason of suicide happens due to financial, health or relationship issues. If the person is lucky, due to some past good karma, he/she may get some relief by family, friends or spiritualistic aides, and get rid of the deadly situation. But, on such circumstances the sufferer long for loneliness, hiding the facts from family, friends, and all known ones.

# HOW TO SOOTHE DEPRESSIVE PSYCHOLOGY OF A PERSON?

Exercise: If find such person. Take the person along with 4 to 5 members of family and well-wisher, or friends to the roof top of the house. Just ask him to imagine the other him (soul) sitting on the veranda of the front house, with sad mood. Counsel him, that this is just for his negativity mindset. Many person face ups and down in life, happy and sad moments, success and failure in life. These are the two sides of a same coin. The most important point is learning positive aspects from such negative results, God teaches us to learn from our own mistake and ahead forward. After this exercise ask him that the other you (soul) of the depressive person return back with smile and no more sitting there. But keep an eye on every movement of the person and find whether he is changing his attitude inside? Also ask him to perform some breathing exercise after getting up from bed in the morning and before going to the bed in the night. Such exercise helps a lot to return the person to normalcy.

# Chapter-21

# DIVINE SLEEP / YOG NIDRA

## What is Divine sleep or Yog Nidra?

On current environ of pandemic, after long self confinement and suffering loss of earning sources, the government decided to reopen the mobility of people and commercial establishments with strict vigilant mode to minimize the causalities. The Government and public both suffered huge financial loss. Mostly daily wagers, service class and entrepreneurs come under tremendous mental pressure. Hence are spending sleepless nights visualizing the darker future ahead. In such situation most of such people encounter mental and physical pressure of life that cause decline in health and mental potentiality. Hence daily practice of Divine Sleep / Yog Nidra proved to be most beneficial to calm down our brain's negative though process.

<u>Exercise</u> - Ask the stressed person to sit on a sofa, or sleep on a bed comfortably. While sit on sofa, Close the eyes rest both palms on the thy or knee, fingers curve naturally upwards,  sit on the sofa; While sleep on bed, put straight both hand on the bed, palms facing upward, fingers curved

upwards naturally. Now, sitting on sofa, just feel your favorite color enters into your toes, from the furs, fills your feet, enters towards your ankles of both feet. Sleeping on bed Feel yourself entered into an bubble ball, full of cool oxygen, that flows on the ocean fare away from the crowd beach. Enjoy divine peace, coolness of the ocean breeze. Feel your favorite color enters upward to your knee, slowly comes towards thighs, waist, stomach, chest, shoulders, and neck. Also feel the cool breeze of the ocean, blue brine water around you. The color now covers to your face and head. Keep feeling such incredible cool that drench you completely as long as you feel comfort with and feel like asleep.

After this exercise will feel mental peace, get a deep slumber all night.

# **GOAL OF LIFE**

<u>What is Goal?</u>: To ask our mind to get a desired result is called Goal. There are two types of goals we try to achieve in life - Short term and long term goals.

A)  Short term goals: In our day to day life we set our daily personal or business goals either in our mental thoughts or by writing the number of goals on a paper or on our personal diary. At the end of the day, we over look the number of goals we achieved, and the rest we carry forward for the next day. For achieving maximum number of goals we get mental satisfaction.

B)  Long term goals: Similarly, we also set some goals to achieve in future like in some days, months or in some years. These are bigger goals by nature. Like clearing the study with excellent grade; getting a job or start a venture in future; get marriage; visiting a foreign country, so on and so forth.

But there are certain divine principles that we have to follow to achieve our goals:

1) Maintain secrecy: we should not disclose our goals or plane of actions for achieving our dream goals to any other person. Because, as per divine principles, once we achieve our goal and get excited, our mind releases Dopamine hormone and close the goal as achieved. Hence, when we explain to our friends and relatives about our goal and feel elated by their encouragement, our brain releases dopamine hormone and closes further proceed on the matter. So be very cautious about managing our goals. Again, after setting a goal, we need to take consistent action to proceed towards our goal as strong and effective.

2) Positive Actions: We need to take stern positive actions to achieve our goal. We must follow our goals as important as our breathing oxygen from the environment.

3) Positivity: We should utter some positive affirmation to achieve our goal. Like, if our goal is to lose weight. Do not utter affirmations like, "I look too much fat, and wish to lose my weight. Rather utter, " I wish to look slim". Because each word we utter on our affirmation, our brain receive on its own language and start acting. So our goal should highlight on our affirmation very positively.

4) Patient: Do not try to test the result of our goal just after few hours, or days of initiating action towards goal.

As we keep a water bottle in the refrigeration to get cool, and start seeing it time to time if got cool or not, it will get

more time to get desired cool, as opening of refrigeration door disturbs the desired cooling system. So be patient, leave on the nature take its own time to fetch the desired result. Hence, perfect conglomeration of all the divine orders only helps us to achieve our dream goal in life.

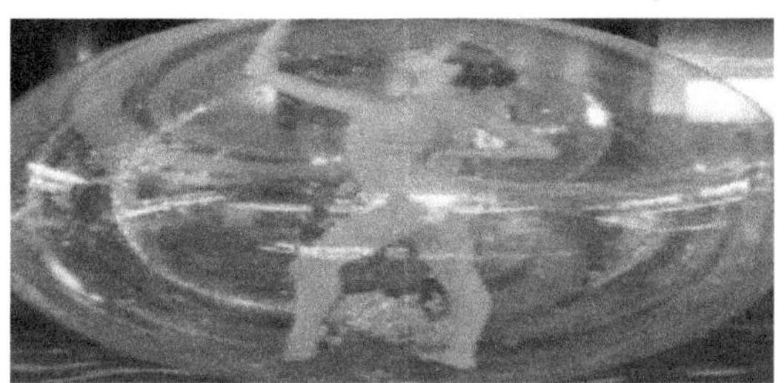

# Chapter-23

# WAYS TO ATTRACT OUR FUTURE GOAL

The Face Book CEO, Mark Zukerberg developed WhatsApp message system to share picture, audio, video and voice message to the person across the globe in no time.

Did he do any labor physically? An emphatic 'No'. One's his system finds in place, for better understanding of the users, he prescribed user's manual to get correction if find anything wrong or malfunctioning. The happening of wrong or malfunctioning is just because of the user's mistake of operation. We never meet Mr Zukerberg physically, but we get enormous benefits of his system.

This is just the tinniest example in compared to the creator of this universe, developer of the invincible mystical principles to manage His unfathomable kinds of creations, which is bay beyond our imagination and thoughts. Gita, Ramayan, Bible, Quran, etc. are the user's manual to know functionality of Creators principles of operation by daily actions. The great thing is that software needs many licensed agreements to operate, but God's manual need no agreement, but strictly punishable in case of misuse of the manual. Please follow under mentioned some manual points of God.

### 1. Fixing Goal:

Like we fix every day our daily routine schedules from getting up from Bed in the morning to going back to bed in the night. We put our glance on our goals achieved and carry forward to next day those goals not completed yet. But these are our daily targets or short term goals.

### 2.   How to set long term goals?:

Set the unbelievable and very big size goal in life. Your goal should be so unique that you should face laughter and criticism from your friend and family circle. But do not care for those negative comments, rather they are only your strength to achieve your desired goal by walking on divine path. Write the points to achieve your goal. And daily revise those points and measure your step forward towards your goal.

### 3. How Law Of Attraction helps to materialize our goals?:

Whole universe is running on a particular law. Newton, the father of science has discovered that all object fall on the ground. It says that we need to put energy to reflect our life. Generally the energy we see, only we believe on those energies. Such energies are called physical energy. But most of our mental energies are not visible but only sensible. As we completely exhausted after long mental work, we feel much pain both in our body and mind. For example, If a soccer player kicks the ball on the right direction, he gets a goal, but a slightest mistake miss the chance.

On our thoughts again and again, our subconscious mind receive the instruction, and direct our body to act to get our result. Hence our mind contains unfathomable energy to produce result. But such results are like walking on the sharp edged a sword. Ehen our energy goes on negative direction and pays us negative result. Hence, only a few people get richer and richer, whereas most people get poorer and poorer. If we visualize such positive thoughts continuously for 21 days, we create result as we desired. If happens immediately, it pays us negative effects in long run, as the true result takes its own time to happen.

How to do Visualization?

Without visualization, it's like trying to drive a car without petrol. Similarly, if we visualize with our clear mind with complete believe and trust, will get sure result. Our goal should synchronize with each atom of our breath that we take into our body, without which we feel lifeless. If our thoughts and visualization are not well synchronized, then no result is possible. So, daily verification of well balance between our thoughts and visualization are as necessary as our food to live our life.

5. <u>What would be the result?</u>:

For example, when we wish to buy a car, we start seeing the similar car around our locality, around our work place and on the road. This is because of our law of attraction. By the time we go to the showroom to buy the car we might be visibly seen the color, style, design of our dream car. Along with visualization, strong consistency action is the real wheel to get nearer to our dream goal. God's intuitive instructions appear when our visualization, action and full-fledged attention are well synchronized, are called divine support.

6. <u>How to convert negativity into positive</u>:

Like skilled software developer develops good software, and before get popularity of the software, the negative group develops many types of anti-virus software to protect the user. So, the negative effects of antivirus software ultimately act as positive help to the original software developer. On the same way, the true goal achiever should take all negative comments around life as indirect support to achieve the dream goal.

7. <u>Conversation with the super power</u>:

Human being lives like stray in such human jungle. Like a child lost his parents in the crowd of a fare, afraid of who will take care of the life? Similarly, many a time, we feel lonely and afraid of our safety and security of our own and family's life. Due to our no faith on the creator of this universe, our brain generates such thoughts. But in real sense, almighty is kind to all, weather lover and hatred to Him. He takes every living being as His own creation, and loves equally. All fear, insecurity and anxieties are of our own creation.

Once we practice His divine principles, we start listening to His intuitive instructions at the time of our wrong choose of path. We feel grateful to His intuitive advice and lead happy and joyful life. To understand His intuitive language, we need to develop 100% faith on Him, without His instruction, we even won't breathe a bit of oxygen. Such intuitive instructions are act like God's response to our message through our daily prayer.

8. <u>Action</u>:

No result can happen without action. Taken action with positive thought to get rich may get long time, but live a peace and happy life. But, to become a rich with negative mindset, like giving or taking bribe to get work done, may get momentary joy and happy, but in long run of life, will have no peace and tranquility. So karmic wealth only goes along us to the next world. This is the simple divine principle.

9. <u>Don't leave the goal on the half path</u>:

If we think that we leave the current job, once we get a better opportunity. The seriousness for better opportunity never comes to us. Hence, we neither leave the current job, neither we get time to apply for better jobs available in the market. And the situation will be to live with the current job though not satisfaction. If anyone wishes to be an IAS officer, but no time to read, universe will take all useless times like girl friend; gossip on social media on mobile; and so on; and avail books, coaching classes, and study atmosphere to reach the goal. So be ready to accept unfavorable changes in life.

10. <u>Understand the loop of our brain</u>:

Many a time we fall into negativity even after our positive actions; don't worry for such moments. This happen because, when we perform positivity, the already over filled mind get empty the negativities those have been already filled since our past many years. So, just tell the brain that whatever is happening negative are of previous karma, and things will change in future on carrying the current job with 100% faith on the God.

11. <u>Affirmation</u>:
<u>Why affirmation is important</u>?

Affirmation means we thank God for whatever He offers us, we accept gracefully and thank Him for the offer. Even any one disturbs during our prayer, during visualizing our goal, or any such achievable task, this is because of our mind only attracting to them, they have no iota of jealousy or irritation towards us. Instead of reacting to them affirm God that these disturbances are of my own attraction to them and help them keep happy. Keep uttering such affirmation daily on pray to the Almighty, the negativity in person around us starts behaving positively. Affirmation gives us strength, energy, and improves our will power.

## 12. How to choose correct affirmation?

Incorrect way uttering affirmation give negative result. For example, if someone need good health. And utter affirmation, "Oh God, I wish to remove sickness from my body." Though the intention of healthy body seeker is not wrong, but our sub-conscious mind picked the word sickness and deletes the rest. And our brain send the message accordingly to the Almighty and fetch a worse outcome. So one should utter, "Oh God give me healthy Physique". Pure positive affirmation to get completely positive results.

## 13. Gratitude:

Gratitude means to show humble respect to everyone- starting from God to devil, from friends to foe, from loved ones to enemies in life. We should not forget every one's efforts to develop our life performance. The utterance of gratitude should come from the core of the heart and not just from outer layer of our mouth. Thanks to each one positively do not negatively associate with the outcome of the result. Serving poor and needy is true gratitude to help others. If pray God to give wealth to help the poor and, on the bus stand if a beggar begs for a coin, and we thought once we fulfill our prayer then can give a coin to this beggar, is not a true gratitude, and the prayer get negative result. Pray should be without any attachment, any lurch or any agreement with the God. Most of the wealthy class never give a coin to any poor or marginalized, but donate hefty amount to the imaginary God installed on the temple. For which, Indian temples are richer then the RBI establishments. This is just because of most of the Indian live a deceptive life; a true gratitude less, but attitude full life.

Like water takes its own time to transform into ice, similarly our prayer also takes its own time to get the result reflected. In-depth patient and faith only get God's blessings.

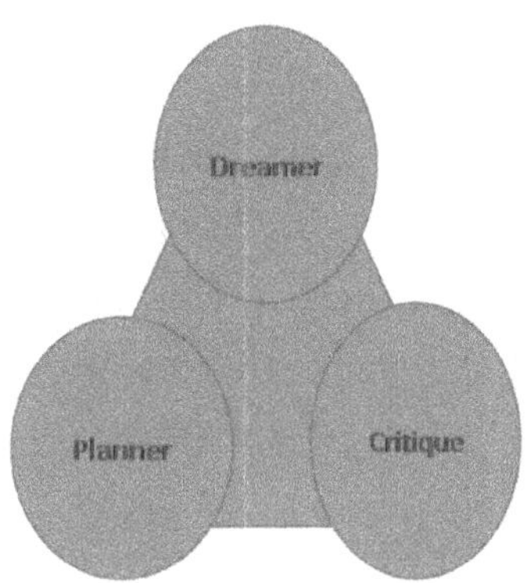


# Chapter-24

## ACHIEVING GOAL – DREAMER, PLANNER AND CRITIQUE EXERCISE

This World of Disney exercise is the most popular to achieve your desired goal successfully. Draw a triangular as shown on the above picture. Also draw three circles on each corner of the triangle.

**Dreamer**: On upper circle write Dreamer means the goal you have fixed to achieve in life. Write on your note pad about how your dream goal is important to you.

**Planner**: The circle on left corner of the triangle helps you plan the steps available for you to achieve dream goal. So write 10 points that you think will definitely help to achieve this goal.

**Critique**: On right corner of triangle the circle of critique. Because, in success of any project critique play major role to get ultimate success to achieve your dream goal.

Now, stand with your goal firm in mind on the dreamer circle. Give your dream goal your favorite color. Close your eyes and feel the color slowly and steadily sheds down from head to face, to neck, to shoulder, to chest, to belly, to waist, to knee, to ankle, to feet and to lower slides to feet, and now spread all over the dreamer circle.

Now shift your step to planner circle. Verify all 10 points you wants take, which you have already mentioned on your note book. Read out all 10 steps, one by one, wish to take in order to achieve your goal, and feel each goal shades from brain and move to the circle.

**Critique**: Now move to Critique circle. And verify all your 10 steps by the critique. On all three circles you act as own dreamer, planner and critique of your goal and step to achieve the dream goal. Now, as critique, ask if any hurdles faced by your steps planned. If ant hurdles arises, then try to change the point. Once confirmed firmly from critique only accept the steps as approved and proceed for action. And now the action taken makes sure to achieve the desired goal.

<u>Now get ready to arrange resources to materialize your dream goal</u>:

Resources like expenses, staff, location, other earning sources, and list of expenses, etc. Because as difficult to achieving dream goal, the more difficult to maintain its consistency and growth in future.

## Corporate Training Through
## Contrastive Analysis (Mirror posture)

This NP exercise is specially meant for marketing and production staff to boost production and sales process. To read psychology of the prospective buyer the sales person should follow points at the time of discussion. For example, if working as sales person in a car show room, just seat opposite to the prospective buyer. Change your sitting style just opposite to the prospective customer, If customer put his right hand on the arm of the chair, you need to put your left hand on the arm of the chair while discussing with the customer. Observe customer's interest in VAK format. If the customer is take visual interest, he will start looking pictures of the car on the brochure, posters hanging on the walls, or throw his glance on the car displayed physically on the show room. If he is interested in audio, will look around the sound of the car or song coming from around the nearby place; if interested in Kinesthetic, will try to touch the pictures on the brochure or physical cars displaying on the show room. Accordingly, the sales person must deal with the customer. For example, after extracting taste of the test of the customer, if interested visual, sales person should visualize the look of the car, the finishing touch of each part of the car; If interested in auditory, show the sound of the engine, horn, silencer, doors, etc.; if customer is interested in kinesthetic, then make him touch each parts of his dream, so that the customer keep interested on your expression, and again bring to sit for final discussion. If the customer is fully impressed with your expression, observe his sitting position changes the way you sit. This means the customer is completely aligned on your way of expression, and 100% made his mind to buy the car from you, for sure.

Similarly, the management can bust the production potentiality of manufacturing unit with such VAK method among the production staff.

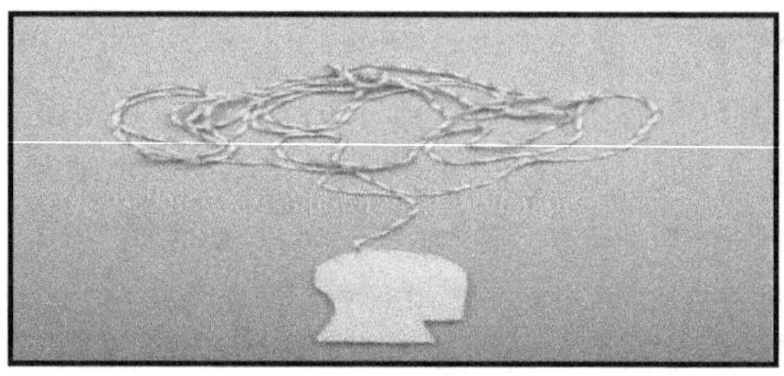

# Chapter-26

# CORPORATE TRAINING OF CHANGING PERCEPTION OF LABOR AND WORKING STAFF (META MODEL)

Change the perception pattern of Executive, clerical and labor class staff. Through this method can alter the negative perceptions already stored can be change by altering through conscious or analytical mind through conversation.

For example, asking questions diplomatically reduce the staffs' generalization point of view of an issue to pinpoint view by following three interventions:

1. **How exactly?**: If the leader of the labor group complaint about the management for not satisfying the labor staff's demand in a general point of view- Ask – "How exactly?"

2. **What exactly?**: If put common bunch of demands, then ask, "What exactly?"

3. **What need to happen for you to know that?**: Means insisting the leader to bring forth the exact proof of the complaint, and convince the group leader that demand is based on general gossip and not based on any proof.

In case of reactive statement from customers by comparison:

A.  Your product is too costly.

i)  Question – Compare to what / who?

B)  Opinion  as fact- Today is very hot.

i)  For home? Is it same bad hot day for cold drink and juice vendors?

C)  Generalization: All politicians are worthless.

i)  According to whom? Not exactly all politicians?

D)  Distortion: Hypnotic language; Milton Model; Unclear artful language.

i)  Set rapport skill.

ii)  Bypass conscious mind (Meta model)

iii) Access unconscious (unclear and hidden)  How to guess potential customer's interest

# MOOD GESTURE & BODY LANGUAGE

| Representation System | Visual | Auditory | Kinaesthetic |
| --- | --- | --- | --- |
| Eye Movement | Defocused, upward right or left | Towards ear/ left down. | Right down |
| Voice | High speed/ High tone | Melodious/ Medium/ Regular Pause | Low deep ton/ Slow, long pause |
| Breathing | High & Shallow | Even Breathing | Deep breathing |
| Posture/gesture | Tension/ Neck extend/ Hard Movement | Rhythmic movement/ Tilted head | Rounded Shoulder/ Head down/ Relaxed muscle |

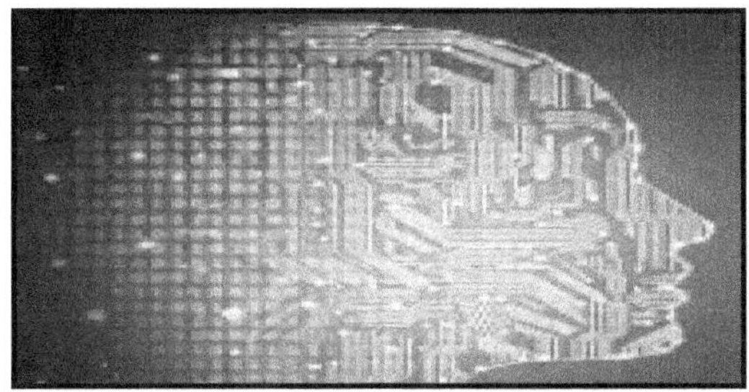

# NEUROLOGICAL ALLIGNMENT

Our life thoughts are based on some divine principles. For example, we got a lottery and purchased the most expensive car of the globe "Lamborghini". But latter find that the car pulls the steering to one side of the road. There is of no use of such expensive car. Similarly, most of the time, we feel useless due to malfunction of our life too.

Our life develops on following steps:

A) <u>Reactive Zones</u>: leading a struggling lifestyle like 97% of common people live on this earth.

1) Environment, influenced by the society around us.

2) Behavior / action by which we respond to others, verbal or non-verbal.

3) Skill and capacity we developed to get our livelihood.

B) <u>Active Zones</u>: USA Former president - Abraham Lincoln, Indian former president- Dr Abdul Kalam, Indian national father – Mahatma Gandhi, who were started very hardship life before reaching to such Himalayan pick position.

4) Believes – Our positive thoughts influenced by our relationship, finance and health.

5) Values – To which we give important - relationship, wealth / money, freedom, commitment, etc. (born with, but lost under the time of social drive).

6) Identity – In order to ascertain ourselves (positive or negative) – Who we are? What meaning we give to our name? Who am I? What's the purpose of my life?
7) Spiritual purpose- To grow self, to contribute to the society around us.

# Chapter-29

# COMPRISION BETWEEN MATERIALISTIC EGO AND SPIRITUALISTIC SOUL

| | |
|---|---|
| Ego seeks to serve itself | Soul seeks to serve others |
| Ego seeks outward recognition | Soul seeks inner authenticity |
| Ego sees life as a competition | Soul sees life as a gift |
| Ego seeks to preserve self | Soul seeks to preserve others |
| Ego looks outwards | Soul looks inward |
| Ego feels lack | Soul feels abundance |
| Ego is mortal | Soul is eternal |
| Ego is drawn to lust | Soul is drawn to love |
| Ego seeks wisdom | Soul is wisdom |
| Ego enjoys the prize | Soul enjoys the journey |
| Ego is cause to pain | Soul is cause of healing |
| Ego rejects God | Soul embraces God |
| Ego seeks to be filled | Soul is eternal wholeness |
| Ego is Me | Soul is We |

 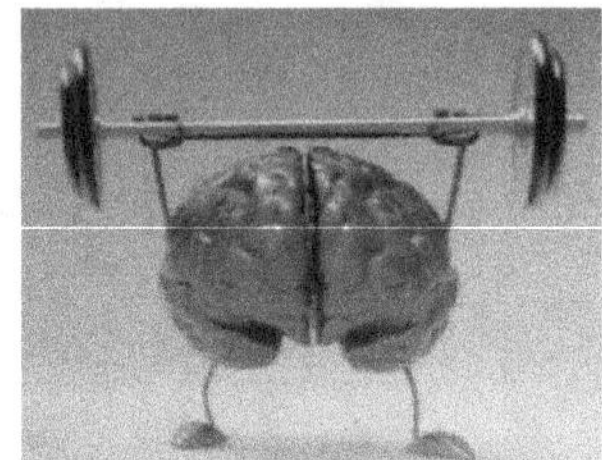

# Chapter-30

# WAYS TO DEVELOP
# GENIUS BRAIN POWER

<u>By practicing A- Z of following good habits</u>

1. Attitude: Positive attitude comes from strong faith in yourself and your capability. If you are happy and view life positively, your brain will be young and healthy.

2. Affirmation: One who wants to develop super brain power may repeat any of the following positive statements:

* My brain is improving day by day.

* Learning and remembering are easy for me.

* My Mind works effectively and efficiently.

* My memory id powerful and alert.

We may also create any such affirmations and repeat will submerge in our subconscious brain and program us to use our brain to the fullest extent.

* Awareness: The three major functions of our brain are thought, feeling and action. The more we attentive towards current events, the easier we can recall these events, as memory in future. Awareness, concentration, focus, mindfulness, alert are the skill of processing and storing information that become memory.

* Calmness: When the negative emotions like anger, irritation, animosity, hatred, etc are present the blood flows to the entire body at a heightened level. On calmness in mind, blood flow focused mainly to brain. This enhances our brain performances.

* Concentration: Concentration alone could double our brainpower. Our healthy brains only concentrate well. It also called as will power.

* Creeping and crawling: A new born baby before walking, start creeping and crawling to make the mind and body stronger. This exercise re-stimulates our mid brain.

* Enthusiasm: We can achieve anything on this world through enthusiasm. Every great achievement is the story of a flaming heart. People or Nature>

* Environment: It may be with people or with nature. Grow a garden, track a mountain, listen raptly to the chirping sounds of the birds, and talk to the stranger without hesitation. The more we cling with the environment, the more we proficient our brain become.

Exercise Physically: Physical exercise or any such functions daily unclog our veins, and make free flow our blood to our heart and mind. Improves our heart functions, reduces our stress and depression level. Along with exercise, swimming, jogging and walking are the best ways to enhance our brain power.

Happy frame of mind: Human brain performs effectively with a happy frame of mind. Being happy or unhappy is our own choice. Un happiness is sometime unconscious invite by our own actions.

Healthy mindset: Living with a healthy mindset always is the source excellent brain functions. Habits like our good attitude towards our circumstances and environment. Utterance of positive affirmation each day.  Positive thinking, healthy diet, drinking of adequate amount of water, empting of bowel every morning keeps us free of constipation, maintain good sound sleep,  use of nature cure, rather depending on avoiding synthetic medicines as much as possible,

Imagination: Positive imagination is as good as meditation which help brain to function well. We can cure 95% of our illnesses by just developing our imagination power effectively.

Intellectual companion and interactive dialogue: Reading spiritual books and attending spiritual discourses fills positive vibes in our brain. All spiritual scripts are works like user's manual of working a computer like brain perfectly. Like the best antivirus pack spiritual discourse refine our brain at least for few days. So, internal reading and attending spiritual discourse prove to be developing effective brain.

Listening to music and other hobbies: Listening to music makes a conscious effort to understand the music and enjoy it, where just hearing refer to the sounds in our surroundings.

Living in present: Present in life should be enjoyable. As the past is dead and the future is unborn. Not living in present with vibrant mood, stress in mind is inevitable by either exploring into past or fearing about future. Guilt of past and worries of the future always haunt each one of us. Only those who know how to grab the present and maximize it have chosen a stress-free life.

Accept the inevitable: All things that are inevitable in life should be accepted gracefully; otherwise we shall be tormented with stress, tension and worries.

We are what we are: We should learn to accept the circumstances we live in. We should not compare with other known ones around us.

Always proud of our uniqueness on this universe: Be proud of our uniqueness on the creation of the God. On this I remind the sayings of famous motivator Dale Carnegie, "Make the most of what Nature gave you. In the last analysis all art is biological. You can sing only what you are. You must be what your experience, your environment and your heredity have made you. For better or for worse, you must cultivate your own little garden, and play your own little instrument in the orchestra of life."

Don't believe in competition in life:   There is no success or failure in life. It is just a matter ou our attitude. We should take life just as it unfolds. We should do our best in life without bothering much about the result. There is no question of failure, it is just to accomplish more attempt to finish the task on hand. We should always utter the affirmation on mind, "When I win, I win, but when I loss, I learn." Ever failure has to be considered as differed success.

Convert negative into positive: List up all positive and successful events happened in the past. Read them every morning just after awake from bed for seven times. Look at the day in the evening how happily it passed away? This is called self positive affirmation.

Don't expect gratitude: On this highly materialistic age, most people have no time to show gratitude after receiving favor from others. So it is better to not expect gratitude for the favor we have offered to anyone.

Follow the stress-free attitude: Whenever we face failure, we should utter, "The best is yet to be." This positive attitude helps us to strive hard to improve our potential, capabilities, efficiency, character, etc.

Meditation Practice: Since yoke, practicing meditation said to be the best medicine for both mind and body to keep fit and fine.   Practicing regular meditation practice develops mindfulness.

Novelty in life: Human brain said to be hungry for new vibes in life. Regular monotonous functions on day to day life makes human brain boor. Hence our ancestors trained us to celebrate some functions or the others in our family, local, national or universal level. Whenever we bring change in pattern of our daily life, our brain functions well to observe that new pattern. Some examples depicted as follow:

As living being we are habituated to function as per instructions from our sense organs. Suppose any one of our organ, say eye is not able to work what change our brain changes? For example taking bath closing eyes, using un habituated hand like a right hander may use left hand while writing, putting clothes, etc; changing your ball pen to ink or gel pen; taking a different route to school or work place, etc; changing dishes – if habituated to South Indian, change to North Indian food; if habituated to eat chilly, change into deserted sweets; change the routes of your morning walk; Visiting a new pace; meeting new people and environment, etc; change spoken to sign language; repositioning of furniture in home or at work place. Change of any such pattern stimulates our brain to reposition its regular way of function and accept extra energy to enhance its functioning.

Reading: Reading is the most effective way to powerfully stimulate both left and right brain. But unfortunately a study find that only 20% of people like to read kooks.

Questioning: Asking questions on whatever subjects we encounter in our day to day life help us to boost our brain power.

Reflexology: It is said that the left brain takes care of the right body and right brain takes care of the left body. When we breathe through our left nostril, our right brain stimulates and vice versa. Similarly, we have access to more brainpower at the tips of our thumbs and big toes. Such therapy is called as reflexology. We can find complete energy map of our body on bottom of our each foot and the palm of each hand. These points of massaging on our hands and feet act as stimulator to our brain.

<u>Example-1</u>: sit on a chair or floor comfortably, keep the right leg on the left thigh. Catch hold of the big toe with right thumb and index finger and massage for three minutes. Similarly, massage all the other toes too. Now do the same act with the left toes. Do such exercise seven minutes each day and feel the magical change of brain power.

<u>Example-2</u>:

a) Half stretch both hands, with widen fingers of both hands. Now, clap both hands in such a way that the space between fingers can heat with other hands' space between fingers. This acupressure points energies our brain and cures some physical deficiencies exists in our body.

b) Stretch the palms of both the hands bend the fingers of both hands to back as much as possible. Now see the mounts on the routes both palms, now clap the palm in such a way that mounts of both the palms hit each other. Doing such exercise for 10 times each morning will help our brain to diagnose our physical deficiencies.

c) Now stretch palms of both the hands. Clap both the palms in such a way that each point of fingers, mounts and hills of the lower palms heat each other. This exercise daily for few minutes will instruct our brain to diagnose defective parts in our body.

There are many more exercises our Indian ancient hermits have discovered for well being of the human kind.

<u>Repetition</u>: With repetition, our neurons become well connected and myelinated to make recall of information easy.

<u>Sex</u>: Studies have shown that sexual stimulations releases endorphins, a type of hormone in the brain and not only eases tension, but also relieves the pain of arthritis and other ailments. Regular sound sex helps us think better.

<u>Silence</u>: Human brain is considered as thoughts manufacturing factory. Since our awake in the morning to going to the bed in the night, around sixty to eighty thousand of thoughts manufactured on our mind daily. But most of them are repetitive. Spending few moments in meditative state keep us away from such restless thought process. Such exercise helps to boost our brain potential.

<u>Sleep</u>: Sound sleep in natural process our body recovers from wear and tear of daily life. Without sleep, we lose much of our ability to transfer the day's information into our long term memories. A short nap after lunch is enough to charge up for the rest of the afternoon. People who hold high positions and those desirous of accomplishing great things in life sleeps less than those who drift aimlessly in life. But, too much of sleep too can slow down brain potentiality.

<u>Thinking</u>: As much as positive thoughts we input to our brain, our brain takes as the great bless from us. Hence, thinking works as best exercise for our brain, as walking works as good exercise for our body.

<u>Travel</u>: travelling to new places and interacting with strangers is a good way to coax the brain to remain active on changing situations. Travel provides abundant opportunity for mental exercise, which is vitally important for brain generation.

Writing: Writing is considered as brain-building exercise. Practicing writing considered as brainpower booster.

Apart from above good habits, there are other ways to enhance our brain potentiality. Some of them are yoga, diet and minerals that helps our brain boost like never before.

<u>By practicing Yoga</u>

<u>Holding the breath</u>: Practice of holding breath during yoga or during swimming enhances brain IQ by 10 to0 15 points, says Dr. Win Wegner, a Japanese scientist on his research.

<u>Simple Meditation</u>: Practicing of yogic asanas like pranayama and meditation are also boost brain concentration. Simply sitting on meditative state about 15 to 20 minutes our subconscious brain receive message that we are in meditation and a sense of self discipline emerges in our brain.

<u>Sabdha (sound) meditation</u>: travel confines us in a particular seat with various sounds. Concentrate entire attention on the sounds coming to mind.

<u>Chitta (consciousness) Meditation</u>: Concentrate on steam of thoughts or feelings. When a thought, feeling and perception, etc are being screened on our mental horizon, just be stay as an ardent observer until it passes out of our visual space. Don't

attempt to explore, follow-up or associate with any of the thoughts or feelings that as passing through our mind.

Visualization: Keep an image or object you love as your supreme God in front of your eye. Visualize it with your closed eyes. When it goes out of your visualization, bring it back and keep it in your consciousness. This practice helps stagnant to your wavering mind. Imagination, will power and eyesight also improve to a great extent.

Zen meditation: Focus on your breathing. When some other thought intrudes, push it aside. Start counting your breathing process – one, two, three, and so on. Your total attention is gently and firmly fixed on the action of counting only. Even counting backward make you more concentrated.

Oil-pulling technique: This technique of ancient India now being scientifically investigated and is considered a panacea for many ailments. The best time of this technique is on the early morning, just after wakeup from bed and before brush your teeth. Take one teaspoon of purified sunflower oil, or sesame (til oil) in your mouth. Gargle for about 20 minute till the oil becomes watery in mouth with foam. Spit out the foamed water and brush your teeth. Mouthy is said to be the gateway to all diseases. This technique prove to the saver of all mouth infections.

Aroma therapy: Our smell sense organ and skin sense organ function like the best brain power boosting act with aroma therapy treatments. The types of aroma conducive for stimulating our brain. Aromas like lavender relaxes our brain and helps it function better.

Almost all meditation should be treated as a way of life rather than a mere ceremony to be performed piously at an appointed time. Instead of brooding over personal problems, concentrate on some constructive activities that bring benefit to humanity at large. Meditation help keep stress-free that stimulates brain functioning.

<u>What is Pranayama</u>: Our intake of breathing from the environment we live is called prana. Indian sages innovated a variety of techniques to draw more prana from the atmosphere. These techniques are called Pranayama. It may be defined as a systematic approach designed to bring perfect control over the flow of prana throught the body by the application of certain methods and techniques achieved through the regulation of physical breathing.

<u>Practice of pranayama</u>: There are numerous ways of practicing pranayama of which I depicted the most effective ones here:

i)   <u>Ujjayi Pranayama</u>: Sit comfortably, inhale through both nostrils, the chin slightly touch the chest bone. There will be a sibilant sound when the air is pass through the neck wall of the mouth. It is highly beneficial for high blood pressure sufferers.

ii) <u>Nadi sodhana pranayama</u>: Sit comfortably with the left hand on the left thigh. The thumb and ring finger should gentle touch each side of the nose to close the left and right nostrils and the index and middle fingers should touch the forehead. Now inhale through the left nostril counting 123, retain counting 123456, than exhale through the right nostril while counting 123456. Repeat the same with other nostril alternatively. Have to continue for 5 to 7 cycles to obtain best result. Right nostril breath activates the left hemisphere of the brain and the left nostril breath activates the right hemisphere. This technique enhances the performance of both the brain hemispheres.

iii) <u>Kapala Bhyarati pranamaya</u>: Sit comfortably on a bed or floor with folded knee, both thighs touching each other. Close both fists with thumb inside and place on the thigh. Inhale in a mild, slow and long manner and exhale quickly and forcibly by contracting the abdomen muscles with a backward push. Do this exercise 20 to 30 times initially and expand to as many times as possible. As benefit, it cleanses respiratory system and nasal passages. It removes asthma problem and strengthen heart function.

<u>Indian ancient principles of meditation</u>:

As the world is witness that meditation and devotion to God is as old as the evolution of this universe. The ancient Indian sages prescribed meditation is the way to interaction with the creator of this universe. It is said that God has incarnated in human form and prescribed their preaching as user's manual, through which a set of guidelines have been prescribed on which each human being to be carry out their live on this universe. Such manuals for Hindus called "Bhagawat Gita", For Christians called "The Bible", For Muslims called "The Quran", and so on.

In Bhagwat Gita, the user's manual of Hindu says that Meditation time should be start at divine hours (Bramh Muharat) that start from 3:40 am to 4:40 am; then start auspicious hours or Subh muharat from 4:41 to 5:40; then starts healthy hours or swasth muharat from 5:41 to 6:40; then starts sick hours or Vimar muharat, starts from 6.41 and onwards, after which the subject live the day unproductively similar to a seek person.

According to Indian ancient sages it is said that the creator of this universe has been operating this universe through His divine computer. All 4.8 million types of species living on this earth, air and water are His creation. He is managing his creation immaculately. He has fixed a GPS-like device invincibly into the body of each living being and keeps record karmic actions of each living being on His computer. Meditation is said to the antivirus software that keeps our human brain-like extension computer free from negative energies, and helps us to live fit and fine up to the end of our life.

But, very few people on this earth are aware of such concealed divine principles and not able to explore the hidden potentiality of free flow of such natural resources.

<u>A-Z of brain storming dietary habits</u>: Diet in every ones life play a vital role to enhance or downgrade our brain potentiality. Eating a well chosen balanced diet is considered to be the brain booster and healthy life, where as uncontrolled and mindless diet said to be we ourselves inviting our darkest future in life and stay disconnected from the society and from our own ones. Intake of fruits and vegetable are considered conducive of good health. Eat when feel hungry and avoid over eating. Drink plenty of water, but at least an hour before or after meals.

<u>Choline</u>: A we advance in age choline level in our body drops sharply. Hence, suffer forgetfulness. Dr Natraj , Co-workers at National Institute of Health, USA, proved that supplement of 10 grams of choline each day keep us balance our memory power.

Fruits: Dates and dried figs add a substantial amount of potassium, calcium and phosphorus to the diet, as well as magnesium, zinc and iron is vital to develop brain support.

Ginger and garlic: These two aromas are considered as the most important ingredients of Indian spices that are globally used now. Ginger helps us to resist from cough and cold, while garlic purifies our blood. Every morning, if taken three cloves of raw garlic with four to five glass of water, will enhance brain potential.

Sugary diets: Out brain need required quantity of sugar level in our blood. Exact level of sugar in our blood elevates our brain's smartness and mood elevator. It can too perk up our memory, concentration, and learning ability. Deficiencies of blood glucose can cause the brain to slow down and malfunction. On the other hand, high level of blood sugar can cause impair brain performance and memory.

Minerals and vitamins: Most minerals and vitamins help our brain perform optimum function.
i) Magnesium: It helps increase the ani-oxidative power of vitamin E. It also maintains the metabolic viability of neurons and also minimizes brain damage.
ii) Selenium: Around 60% of brain is composed of fat. Selenium prevents oxidation of fat, hence boost immunity and improves circulation. The selenium levels in the blood typically decline 105 by the age of 60. Hence 50 to 100 gm daily intake of selenium can keep our brain fit and fine.
iii) Manganese: The most effective for forgetfulness of our brain. 1 to 9 mg of intake each day helps produce thyroxin in the thyroid gland.

Vitamin: Vitamin B, C and E are said to be the main brain boosters.

Vitamin B: Vitamins are also help boosting our brainpower. Vitamin B (B1, B 13, B6 and B12) are the proved as the igniters of brain power. Such vitamins are frequently discharged from our body, hence regular intake help replenish such vitamin deficiencies.

Vitamin C: Vitamin C helps concentrating high level of brain tissue and contributes to the creation of neurotransmitters, such as dopamine, and protects cells from free radical damage, also protect against age related brain degeneration, including Alzheimer and brain stroke.

Vitamin E: Vitamin E is much available in selenium, as already explained on mineral section above. It helps reduce brain stress process.

Apart from the above brain boosters, there are other play-way methods to keep our brain function enhanced are playing Carom, Chess, Sudoku, Crossword, etc.

# Chapter-31

# WHY THE LIVING BEING SPINNING ON DEATH AND BIRTH CYCLE?

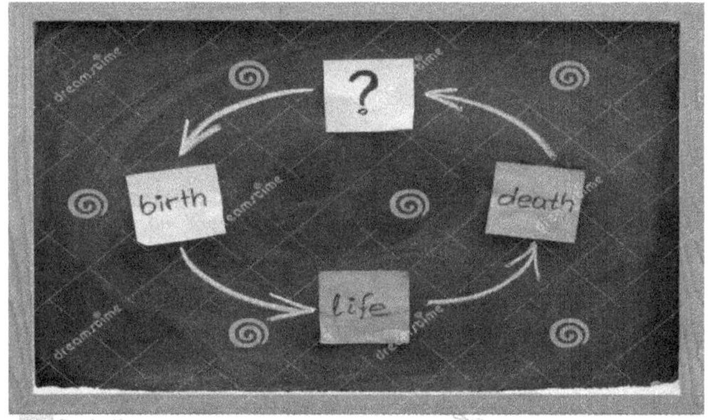


Either any living being, especially human being that considered to be the nearest to the creator, still face the creator's invincible rule of swirling on birth and death cycle of life. This is because the creator has no differentiation to any of His subjects. Each one has to either suffer or reward according ones karmic cause and effects. Hence the major principle of divine is until one fulfill his/her desire before leaving from this mundane earth, has to come back to get fulfill ones unfulfilled desire.

<u>The following karmic table may explain this better</u>: Like we human beings are well aware of three traffic lights. The middle orange light always advise to judge whether you are doing legal or illegal while crossing. The above instruct us to move safe and save life. On the other hand the lower red light strictly warns us to stop heading further. In spite such mechanical warning most riders cross the traffic light and cause hazardous to other fellow travelers, for which insure desirable penal punishment. Similarly, though the divine principles are not mentioned anywhere, such user's manual of spiritual principles are available on holly scripts of each religion, like "Bhagwat Geeta" for Hindus; "Bible" for Christians; "Quran" for Muslims; and so on.

But the human, being the DNA of apes, mostly act like copycat, very few are use their mind in innovative way and move to spiritual path by offering their action for the wellbeing of the larger mass of the society.

SPIRITUAL PATH: Many feel following spiritual path is not east, many of the human species dose not know about spirituality. But it is no other than just polishing our regular karmic actions. Rather we can say that just reversing our daily karmic actions mentioned on our lower path is the main understanding to spirituality.

1. Practicing giving up our selfishness, showing our gratitude to every living and non living being around us; give up negative feeling or discussion towards every one. Even towards enemy.

2. Practice giving up negative verbal expression or fights towards any living or non living being around us. Even towards our enemy.

3. Practice to avoid physical fight, lurch on others wealth or any

such illegal activities. Rather, donate to the needy and marginalized ghetto of the society. The invincible divine principle is follow the principles, "Service to human kind is to service to God". And you will be pay back 1000 times once do such benevolent actions with serene mind. The glaring example of Bill Gates, CEO of Microsoft, Jeff Bezos, CEO of Amazon, Mark Zukerberg, CEO of Face Book, and so on have donated substantial part of their earning.

4. Rather blood thirsty and criminality mindset that drive to the lowest grade causing untimely and painful exit and get lower grade on next life. Practice social work, mass benevolent service with pure mind to get the highest grade life during or next life.

KARMIC PATH: Human being has been upgraded after experiencing many layers of lives out of 4.8 million types species created by the creator of this universe, with God's expectation of absolve from suffering-full birth and death cycle and dissolve in the ocean of divinity. Now look at why more and more human being fall prey to lower path and even lower the life path of next life. On the other hand the same human being, by ones spiritual karmic path either upgrade the next life path or get mature enough to absolve from cycle of birth and death and completely dissolve in the ocean of divinity.

The silver-line of lower path karmic actions: Though the flower grade of lower path defined as under, but there is a silver-line drawn on the intention of the act performed. For example, if a soldier kills the enemy side personnel with intention to save the country, or any body kill the wild animal to save ones own life is not considered as illegal karmic action.

LOWER PATH: Most of us ignore our human attitude towards others around us and suffer from following grade according to our level of karmic actions.

1. Mental though of selfishness; discriminating towards other living beings; negative feeling or discussion towards other living

beings.

2. Verbal fight and angry expression towards other living beings around the society.

3. Physical fight; theft; acquire others wealth illegally; involve other such criminal activities.

4. This last grade of human being belong to the DNA of animal and blood thirsty creature of last life. Due to extinguish of substantial part of forest and living creatures just to expand human base most of the soul of such wild creatures took their birth on human form, and continue to perform as per the past life DNA. Hence more and more terrorists, blood thirsty and criminal elements raised their hydra head on current times.

9 798869 529529 0